HOW TO TALK TO STRANGERS
~ A STEP-BY-STEP GUIDE TO PROFESSIONAL NETWORKING ~

By:
TAMMY L. TURNER

To: Tony!
May the words on these pages assist you in growing your business relationships!

Cheers,
Tammy
7/2011

How to Talk to Strangers:
a step-by-step guide to professional networking
© 2010 Kapstone Publishing, P.O. Box 2054,Dearborn, MI 48123

Contributors:
Editor: So It Is Written, LLC
Cover Design: Ivory Coast Media
Interior Design: My Vision Works Publishing
Photograph for Cover Design: Robyn Robinson Photography
Make-up for Cover Photograph: Talya Ashford
Hair for Cover Photograph: Andre Healey-Salon Jacqueline & Spa

Printed in the United States of America.

ISBN: 978-0-615-41939-8

Library of Congress Cataloging-in-Publication Data
Turner, Tammy

1. Networking
2. Business
3. Social Media

CONTENTS

Dedication

This book is dedicated, first and foremost, to my Mom, Linda.
Thank you for instilling in me the spirit of a fighter.
Thank you for all that you have done over the course of the years and all that you continue to do.
You are the epitome of strength.

To Noel, Douglas, Omari and Jabari. I love you.

To my NABA family, thank you for giving me the springboard needed to flourish in my career.
I will always strive to live our motto:
"Lifting as We Climb"!

To Keya
Thank you for ALWAYS supporting me.
Saying that you're my best friend couldn't possibly describe all that you've been to and for me. I love you.

To all my "girl" friends and "guy" friends and Facebook family.
Thank you for believing in me, supporting me and encouraging me throughout the years.

To Walter Smith, thank you for your support and encouragement. No periods, only commas!

To my ZamZuu family
I'll see you at the top, in the winner's circle!

Cheers,
Tammy

Don't be pushed by your problems; be led by your dreams.
~ Anonymous

Networking Is...

1: the exchange of information or services among individuals, groups, or institutions; *specifically*: the cultivation of productive relationships for employment or business.

~ Merriam-Webster Online Dictionary

Introduction

Throughout my career, I've noticed that people desire to learn the art of networking. The masses would agree that networking is a skill set that can be utilized to further your career or businesses. What I've also noticed is that many people don't know how to effectively network and therefore, they don't. Educating and enabling individuals to be successful in their career endeavors was my motivation for writing this book.

My passion for networking began many years ago. It happened by accident actually. I guess you could say that I was blindsided or that we sort of found each other and the love affair began. At the very beginning of my career, I never thought about networking, nor did I receive any guidance or attend any classes on the subject while in college. I didn't come from a family of professional networkers either, so I didn't have any guidance from home as it relates to establishing, building, nurturing and maintaining professional relationships.

While in college and early in my career in Corporate America, I would hear colleagues talk about networking and I had no idea what they were speaking of, much less how it could be used to build relationships and possibly advance my career. Although "Networking is the single most effective tool used to advance a person's career," isn't it amazing that it's not being taught in schools, with the exception of one or two schools here and there? As valuable as networking is, one would imagine that it is taught in business schools, at a minimum, as a part of the curriculum.

It's almost as if networking is a secret society. It's the fine print that no one reads or the unspoken rules of the company. You know the ones that everyone is aware of, yet they're not in the employee handbook anywhere. Finally, the networking secrets of the successful are revealed.

I've been actively practicing, teaching and learning the art of networking for approximately 12 years now. What I've attempted to capture in this book is what I've learned over the course of these past 12 years. Some of it may seem like common sense to you, and yet some information may cause you to have an "Ah-Ha" moment.

The techniques outlined in this book are good for the novice networker, the college student, the introvert and even the more experienced, seasoned professional. There's something for everyone, no matter where you are in your college years or professional career.

My challenge to you is this: Take the information that you learn in this book and apply it immediately, and watch how quickly your network will expand. Take stock of the meaningful relationships that you will establish and how fulfilling those relationships will be for all parties involved.

My hope for you, the reader, is that the words on these pages provide you with the guidance that you need to take your career or business to the next level. I hope that you enjoy this book as much as I have enjoyed sharing it with you.

What the mind can conceive, it can achieve.
~ Napolean Hill

1

Don't Talk To Strangers

From as far back as I can remember, when I was but a small child, these are the words that my mom said to me every morning on my way to school. Most of my friends' parents told them the same. This was, obviously, for our safety. However, as you aware, anything that the mind receives in repetition it will internalize. This concept was no different.

As children, we needed to heed these words from a safety perspective; however, as adults we need to GET RID OF THIS THINKING. As mentioned previously, networking is the single most effective tool used in advancing your career (whether self-employed or working for a company). However, how effective can we be at networking if we're not talking to strangers? My challenge to you is for you to change your thinking. Strangers are your newfound best friends!!

Strangers are resources. Strangers are friends. Strangers are connections. Strangers are money in the bank. Yes, that's right, money in the bank. As you begin to master the Art of Networking, with practicing how to engage strangers and other relationship building tools that you will learn in later chapters, you will begin to turn those relationships into revenue for yourself and those in your network. Now, although revenue isn't the sole reason for building and expanding your network, it certainly is a motivator! Wouldn't you agree?

Before we can learn how to network, we must first overcome the *fear* of networking. Many have not experienced success in the area of networking because fear is the motivator behind them not moving forward and executing the plan. This isn't specific to networking; it is true throughout other aspects of our lives as well. We fear what we don't know. Fear paralyzes us, limits us, and makes us stagnate. This is not productive and does not lead to the road to success.

So, if we know that fear has such an adverse effect on us, why don't we just meet it head-on, face-to-face, nose-to-nose, toe-to-toe and say, "TODAY, I TAKE MY LIFE BACK! I WILL NO LONGER ALLOW FEAR TO PARALYZE ME, PARALYZE MY MOVEMENT, MY THOUGHTS, MY ACTIONS OR MY DREAMS! TODAY I TAKE CONTROL, I TAKE MY POWER BACK!"

There… now don't you feel better already?

Let's take a look at what it is about networking that causes fear. Is it fear of rejection; fear of not knowing what to say; fear of not being able to be articulate; fear of not fitting in; fear of having to be social; fear of not feeling like you're as smart or as quick-witted as everyone else? Do ANY of those fears have ANYTHING to do with networking? Absolutely NOT! None of these fears specifically relate to networking. I'm not suggesting that they're not real. I am suggesting, however, that the *thought* of networking did not bring these fears about.

If you fear rejection, that fear will manifest itself in any situation where you have one-on-one dialogue with someone that you don't already consider a close friend. For example, the thought of rejection will rear its ugly head in the following situations: a job interview; male/female relationships; talking to your current boss about that well-deserved raise; a sales call; and the list goes on and on. If rejection is the thought that you are holding on to, you will most certainly make that thought manifest into a reality for you (Law of Attraction). However, the opposite is true. If you maintain pleasant thinking and positive energy, it will boost your confidence and you will cause your positive thoughts to manifest into a reality.

Let's face it; no one wants to be rejected, right?

I want you to take a moment and think about a time where you had to overcome your fear of something in order to move forward and progress. It could have been fear of heights, insects, animals, tests, meeting your future in-laws, or even a job interview. What did you do to overcome that fear? Now, although I don't know you or your personal circumstance, I have a pretty good guess as to what you may have done to overcome the fear in that situation. In order to overcome the fear, you made A DECISION. That's right, A DECISION! You

15

decided that you would no longer be paralyzed by the fear of that thing. When you resolved within yourself that you were not going to be afraid, you made an attempt to get to the other side of that fear. That's 3/4 of the battle. You made a conscious decision to move confidently toward your goal. Use that same mindset and conviction when dealing with your fear of networking. Make a decision to no longer be afraid and move confidently to get to the other side of your goal, which is to expand your existing network.

Several years ago when I was working in Corporate America, actually my first job in Corporate America, I recall being invited to a team outing. The firm that I worked for had many different divisions and teams and was pretty high on networking outside of the office to build morale. At that time, I was NOT the social butterfly that I am today. I dreaded the very thought of going to the team outing. I knew my colleagues at the office and that was the extent of where I wanted our relationship to go. I didn't want to go, not because I didn't like my colleagues, but because I was afraid of networking with them outside of work. In the office, we had plenty to talk about; plenty of work that is. But attending the team outing would place me in a social situation that frankly scared the heck out of me.

Guess what I did? I made a DECISION to go the team outing and at least give it a shot. What did I have to lose? We went to a facility where we were able to play Whirlyball. I had never even heard of Whirlyball, much less knew how to play it. However, I was not deterred. I went to the event and had an opportunity to engage my colleagues in a social setting that was much more relaxing and comfortable than the "play-by-the-rules" of the office.

I had a phenomenal time networking with my colleagues. I learned so much about them, which helped me to adapt to their personalities and for them to adapt to mine. I had such a great time that I never missed another team outing. In fact, I joined the planning committee to organize them through-out the year. I guess you could say... that's all she wrote. I was hooked on networking from that moment on. That's when our love affair began...

If you never aim for it, you'll never achieve it! Set your sights high and Let's Go!!
~ Tammy L. Turner

2

30- Second Elevator Speech

If you have heard anything about networking, you have heard people use the term 30-Second Elevator Speech or Pitch. Everyone, whether they are a professional or student, needs to have a 30-second elevator speech. In essence, this speech gives you an opportunity to introduce yourself to a perfect stranger and give them information about your company or business that will allow for a follow-up at a later date.

If you were in an elevator with Oprah, Bill Gates, Donald Trump, or Will Smith, and you are at the top floor of the Sears Tower or Renaissance Center, what would you say to them? How would you ensure some type of follow-up before your opportunity arrived at their designated floor and opportunity walked out of the elevator?

Wouldn't you agree that it would be beneficial to have something already rehearsed in your mind to articulate to them, other than "I love your work"? This is where your speech comes in. There are 4 components to this speech:

1. Identify who you are (name).
2. Identify your business (name of your business or company that you work for).
3. Identify what you do (CPA, Recruiter, Entrepreneur, Teacher, etc.).
4. Determine what your need is or how they can be a resource to you or how you can be a resource to them.

One might think that this is quite a bit of information to cover before those elevator doors open up. Keep in mind, this is meant to be short and sweet and help you to secure a business card for follow-up at a later date. This is NOT the time to give your resume, certifications, educational background, or other credentials. This is the time to introduce yourself and your business or the service that you offer ONLY.

While I used the above celebrities as an example, you will probably use this speech more often with the people you network with within your school, your industry, your office, or your church. The more that you practice your speech, the easier it is for it to rattle off your tongue with ease. Practice also helps prevent nervous jitters that most people experience when meeting and greeting strangers for the first time and trying to figure out *what* to say to them. Practice makes perfect.

Let's examine what a sample elevator speech would sound like:

Hello, my name is Tammy Turner. I am the President & CEO of Kapstone Recruiting & Training Services. I specialize in the permanent and temporary placement of Finance & Accounting Professionals, as well as Training & Development in the areas of networking, resume writing, interviewing skills, entrepreneurship, and business etiquette. I am also the author of "How To Talk to Strangers ~ A Step-by-Step Guide to Professional Networking". How may I be a resource to you or your business?

I addressed each component of the elevator speech.

1. I identified myself and my title.
2. I identified my company.
3. I identified what I do.
4. I ended with a question that would initiate or encourage further dialogue, either at that very moment or with the exchange of business cards and a follow-up at a later date.

Keep in mind, this is an opportunity for you to sell yourself, your business, or organization. If you own multiple businesses or you have multiple organizations that you belong to, you may want to have more than one elevator speech. You may want to have two or three that are specifically tailored for the audience (person) that you are attempting to connect with.

Your elevator pitch can be altered as many times as you like to cover your updated needs or resources. I would encourage you to practice with someone, and time yourself. Sometimes, we don't realize when we're rambling or our thoughts are flowing in our head smoothly, but when they come out of our mouths, it's a different story. I would also encourage you to call your answering machine or leave a message for yourself on your cell phone. You can also record your 30-second elevator speech with a hand-held recorder. This will help you critique yourself and address any areas of weakness, such as how many times you say the phrase "Umm" or lack confidence or passion in your voice.

If you are not convincing, passionate, and ON ABSOLUTE FIRE about yourself, how can you expect the person that you are pitching yourself or your business to be?

If we all did the things we are capable of doing, we would literally astound ourselves.
~ Thomas Edison

3

How to Initiate Conversation

Throughout the years, and many workshops, training, and seminars, I've discovered (from my participants) that one of the biggest fears about networking is actually how to initiate conversation. Most people are uncomfortable walking into a room full of strangers and engaging them in conversation. Walking up to someone in line at the grocery store, at the basketball game, or at the gym can seem awkward at times. But, this seems to be especially true in a professional setting where someone's professional title is oftentimes an intimidating factor.

This chapter will discuss techniques to engage a person in conversation. First, find the common bond. If you are at a networking event, your common bond would be that particular event. For example, I belong to the National Association of Black Accountants, Inc. (NABA). I have traveled across the country attending various NABA events over the course of my 12 years with the organization. Each year, I see new faces. Being the networker that I am, I want to meet these new faces and see how I can be a resource to them or how they may be a resource to me. So, I walk up to them and introduce myself. These are perfect strangers, BUT we have a common bond. That common bond is that we're both at this particular NABA event. There's also a high probability that this individual is currently a member of NABA or considering membership within the organization.

So my approach in this type of situation is to simply identify the person(s) that I wish to meet and approach them by asking, "*Is this your first NABA Convention or NABA event?*" That's it! Plain and simple. Their response will tell me where to go next with the conversation. If it is their first NABA event, I will ask them how they've enjoyed it so far. Because I have been in NABA for so many years, I will ask them if they have any questions that I may answer for them. If this isn't their first NABA function, and they are already a member, I ask them what chapter they belong to, how long they have been involved in NABA, and what company they work for.

Now that wasn't so bad, was it?

In addition to the common bond approach, I also have other tools in the tool box that are just as effective, such as current events, sports, compliments, and the weather. Yes, as boring as it may sound, it's an age-old conversation starter. Use it! Most people watch the news or read the newspaper in an effort to stay abreast of the happenings locally, nationally, and internationally. These current events are great conversation starters. It would be pretty difficult for you to contribute to a conversation about the earthquake in Haiti or the Tsunami in Southeast Asia if you have never heard about it. In fact, you would probably feel isolated because you would find that you're the only person that hasn't heard about it.

This also levels the playing field. Everyone, no matter what their position in life or business, can have a discussion about current events. It doesn't matter if you're an executive for Ford or a secretary at an Elementary School, you can contribute to a conversation about current events. So, make time to watch the news (not just the local news), read the newspaper, or go online to various news blogs. But find some way to obtain world and local information.

Sports are another conversation starter, especially when talking with men. Yes, ladies, learn to love sports. Most men that I have encountered have a passion for sports. So I find it very easy to initiate a conversation about football (I might add that I'm a die-hard football fan. Go Philadelphia Eagles!), basketball, hockey, or golf. This is especially easy to do during the playoffs. You can engage someone all day long talking about the Superbowl, who you think will win, and why you think they'll win. Even better, if you reference a team's statistics or participate in a fantasy football team, you are well on your way to establishing a relationship! You have now identified a common bond and have engaged in dialogue that has been relaxing for both parties. This is the beginning of a relationship.

Compliments are a great conversation starter as well, especially when they're sincere. People love to hear good things about themselves. I love it when someone gives me a compliment on how well my workshop or seminar went, how nice my suits, shoes, and handbag looks, or even my hairstyle. It says that someone noticed me. Knowing how these accolades make me feel, I don't mind giving them freely and often. I want people to feel good about themselves and it's a great way for me to begin conversation with them.

For example, I'm in line behind a lady at the grocery store. She has on a stylish pair of boots that I absolutely love. I have no problem saying to her, *"I love those boots. They really look nice on you with that jacket. May I ask where you purchased them from? I've been searching high and low for some boots like that and I haven't been able to find any."* Just like that, I've engaged her in conversation by paying her a sincere compliment and making an inquiry that would require further dialogue. Now imagine that we were at a networking event and I approached someone with that same conversation starter. You can see how that would engage the person and inspire further dialogue. After she has provided me with information on where I can purchase the boots from, I will then ask her about the common bond--the event that she and I are at together.

Now, think back to a time when someone approached you at a networking event or a time that you observed someone approaching people at networking events. What did they do to engage you or the person that they approached? What did they say? What did their body language convey?

Were they friendly? Did they smile a lot? Was their introduction smooth and non-threatening?

Here's a learning opportunity for you. If you've ever been approached by someone and you admired their style, COPY IT! Tweak it of course to fit your personality, but incorporate their body language and verbiage. Then practice, practice, practice.

Think about someone whose style, poise, or technique that you admire. Observe them in their element and make a concentrated effort to mimic that behavior. For example, there was a lady that I used to work with in my public accounting days named Ann. She was a sharp lady indeed! I observed her movement and the ease at which she was able to speak with everyone from partners and admins to mail clerks and executives. She was very confident, but not cocky. I admired her style. I saw that she was able to cross the color line barrier and engage professionals and initiate conversation with anyone on any level, even if they didn't look like her. I said to myself, *"That's what I want to do. That's how I want to interact with people.* I began to observe her behavior and I mimicked it, with my own twist added, of course. I wasn't trying to become Ann; I just wanted to emulate some of her behavior traits that appeared to be successful for her in her interaction with others.

Many years later, I shared with Ann how much I admired her style and how I learned early on that having a personality like that could propel my career. Ann and I are close friends to this very day.

We've discussed different techniques to engage someone in conversation, but say for instance that you see a group of people in the midst of conversation. Would you feel comfortable walking up to the group, introducing yourself, and asking to join the conversation? If not, let's discuss a technique that may help you gently ease your way into the group and ultimately, into the conversation, without appearing to be intrusive.

If you're at a networking event and you see a group of people having a conversation, consider approaching the group and saying to them, *"Wow, this looks like a fun (or interesting) group. I saw you guys when I came in. Do you mind if I join you? My name is Tammy."* This is non-intrusive and the group is flattered that you complimented them on being fun or interesting. Therefore, you've broken the ice and created a sense of ease among those in the group. You take this one step further by introducing yourself, and then go to everyone in the group and extend your hand and ask their name. After you get the names out of the way, one of two things will happen: either someone in the group will ask you about yourself, or they will resume the conversation where they left off.

This chapter has given you many techniques to choose from in your efforts to engage a stranger or a group in conversation. The rest is up to you. Practice, practice, practice. Keep in mind, if you interact with someone that seems to have a sense of ease in how they approach someone (a good indicator would be if they were able to successfully engage you in conversation), then mimic their behavior or at the very least, learn from it.

Networking Challenge:

1. During the course of your day today, engage two strangers in conversation using one of the methods outlined in this chapter. It doesn't matter if the two strangers are at a networking event or while you are out engaged in your day-to-day activities.

2. Observe someone that you feel has a sense of ease in approaching and engaging strangers in conversation. Or, observe the way in which someone has engaged you in conversation. Make a mental note of the things you liked and those that you didn't like. The next time you're at a networking event, implement one or two of the new techniques that you learned.

The most important thing about goals is... having one.
~ Anonymous

4

How to Properly Use Business Cards

In today's society, everyone has a business card. The hairdresser, the baker, the candlestick maker and even the little girl selling Girl Scout cookies; everyone has a business card (or at least they should). When my daughter was 17 years old, she created her very first business card to promote something that she was selling in school. From a networking standpoint, business cards are an extremely important tool if used effectively. However, most people don't use business cards effectively, much less for the purpose in which they were intended.

When I discuss business cards at my seminars, I draw a picture for all of the participants in the room of how they go to a networking event, collect business cards, then return to work the next day and put the business cards, with the current stack that they already have with the rubber band wrapped around it, in their top desk drawer. If they're really sophisticated, they have a business card holder that they put the business card into and then stick in the top desk drawer. In order to be effective networkers, we MUST break this bad habit!

The business card is your best friend. Would you throw your best friend in the drawer and forget about him or her? Would you only reach out to them when you needed something? Or would you follow up with them from time to time, just to see how they're doing? When you're at any event where you exchange business cards, you must see that business card as the start of a relationship and in some cases, as revenue.

When I accept someone's business card, I typically write on the back of the card (after they have walked away) something significant about them that will help me remember them, which will aid me in my follow-up email I will send to them. For example, if, during our conversation, they shared something personal about themselves (i.e., family or professional achievements), I write that information on the back of their card to enable me to include it in my follow-up email. If they told me that they just passed all four parts of the CPA exam on the first sitting, that their daughter just participated in a cheerleading competition, or that they are celebrating their 10th wedding anniversary, I will include that information when I send them an email.

My initial follow-up email would go something like: *"Hi Bob. It was a pleasure to meet you at this year's NABA National Convention. It was great meeting so many professionals in the industry from various cities and diverse backgrounds. Let's stay in touch. Please let me know if I can be a resource to you. By the way, how did your daughter's cheerleading competition go?"*

Now when Bob reads this email, he will be taken aback that I remembered his mention of his daughter's cheerleading competition. This is a personal touch that creates a bond. He will remember me at next year's NABA Convention because I created a personal connection with him versus the generic email that lacks personality. Bob may have received a dozen follow-up emails after the convention, but how many of them had a personal touch?

Ask yourself how you would be impacted by an email that was clearly personally directed to you and not a generic email that was mass distributed to you via BCC (blind copy) function of email. When someone sends me a follow-up email after attending one of my seminars, and they reference football or specifically the Philadelphia Eagles, I feel really good about that. It tells me that they were completely engaged in the conversation and were genuinely interested in what I was talking about and what is important to me. Everyone likes to feel special. One way to make someone feel special is for them to know that you actually listened to them and that you take an interest in what's important to them.

My preference for the first contact is via email. It's non-intrusive and it allows the receiver to engage on their terms and in their time frame, which makes a person feel that they're in control of the progression of the relationship. They can respond at their leisure, have an opportunity to compose their thoughts, and respond accordingly. However, depending on the nature of the dialogue when the business card exchange took place, a call may be more appropriate.

At networking events, business cards are exchanged. That implies that you are not only receiving business cards, but that you are also giving out business cards. Now that you know what to do when you receive a business card, let's discuss how your business card should look. Your business card should incorporate the following information:

- Your Business Name
- Your Name
- Your Title
- Your Phone Number (If applicable, office and cell)
- Your Fax Number (if applicable)
- Your Email Address (preferably a business email address and not a personal email address)

I have included additional information on the back of my business cards that will allow the recipient to connect with me via other avenues, such as:

- My Facebook page (TammyTurner PageOne)
- My Twitter page(TamTurn)
- My Blog (http://www.kapstonejobs.blogspot.com)
- My Radio Show (http://www.blogtalkradio.com-kapstonerecruiting)

With the wave of social media dominating how people communicate these days, I want to ensure that you can connect with me via various avenues, and also patronize my work (through radio, public speaking, or my blog) or business. Almost every business owner has a Twitter and Facebook page nowadays. From CNN and Ponderosa, to KPMG and NABA, everyone is utilizing social media. Don't be left behind!

Please ensure that your business card is visually appealing. I'm not suggesting something outrageous, unless you're a graphic designer and you're using an out-of-the-box theme to market your creativity. Your business cards should not look like you made them up on your home computer. Your cards should be professional and printed on quality stock paper. Your business cards ARE a representation of YOU! What do (or will) your cards tell the recipient about your personal brand? The intended purpose of a business card is to provide contact information. The purpose of providing contact information is to encourage continued interaction in an effort to build a professional relationship. Don't be a business card "collector". Be in the business of building relationships, with the card serving as the basis for continued communication, and the first step in the process.

There's no "next time"... Do It Now! It's now or never!
~ Anonymous

5

The 48-Hour Rule

The 48-Hour Rule is a phrase that I created back in 2001. At the time, I was working for Arthur Andersen and I was heavily involved with the firm's recruiting efforts. Simultaneously, I also held a leadership position within NABA that required me to interact, via workshops and seminars, with accounting and finance students. I had begun to notice a pattern of inconsistency with the students at various recruiting fairs that I attended on behalf of Arthur Andersen.

While all of the students took my business card and expressed an interest in employment with Arthur Andersen, not all of them followed up with me after the initial conversation. Of the students that did follow up, the timeframe in which they followed up varied greatly.

Some students followed up the next day, while some followed up two to three days later. Some even took a week or more to reach out. There was absolutely no consistency.

From my interaction with the NABA students after one of my Elements of Success seminars, I realized one of the common questions asked was, "When should I follow up? How soon after the event or initial interaction should I reach out to the recruiter or professional that I met?"

From both my interaction at Arthur Andersen and NABA, I determined that these students should be given a consistent message as it relates to following up with individuals that they have made contact with at a networking event or career fair. As a result, birth was given to the 48-Hour Rule.

The 48-Hour Rule is simple, within 48 hours of meeting someone at an event where there has been an exchange of business cards, you should reach out to that person and make contact. The premise here is that the person is still fresh in your mind, and you are hopefully, still fresh in their mind as well.

The method of follow-up may vary depending upon the conversation that took place during the exchange of business cards. However, the length of time that lapses between the exchange and the follow-up should be consistent.

I have attended many conferences over the course of my professional career, and one thing that people will always tell you is that within 48 hours of meeting me or within 48 hours of my returning from the conference, they received an email or phone call from me in an effort to follow up on our initial conversation. Being consistent in this practice is what helped me to expand my network.

Should you choose to follow up via email, please include information that you wrote down on the back of the business card to help you remember the individual that you spoke with. This will help jog your memory if you've been at an event and interacted with 25 or more individuals.

Once you get in the habit of doing this, practice consistently. It will become second nature to you.

It's not what you know, it's who you know.
~ Anonymous

6

Follow Up and Follow Through!

Engaging strangers is the hard part. Now that you've gotten that out of the way, you should feel a slight sigh of relief. But, it's not over yet. The hardest part of the networking interaction is behind you, but now the real work begins.

Now that you've overcome your fear and introduced yourself to someone new, it's time for you to build and nurture the relationship. Start by sending the individual that you met a follow-up email (assuming they have an email address on their business card). Acknowledge that you enjoyed meeting them at the event or that you enjoyed chatting with them. (Keep in mind the 48-Hour Rule that we discussed in detail in the previous chapter.) You want to connect with the individual while the memory of the conversation is still fresh.

Oftentimes, this is where we miss the boat in the networking scheme of things. Most individuals make contact, but never follow up and as result they don't build or nurture the relationship. Therefore, they lose the opportunity to *be* a resource or *gain* a resource. You never want to come across as the person that only calls when he or she wants something. The way to avoid this distinction is to follow up regularly with your network and take a genuine interest in them and the things that are important to them. Build, nurture, and maintain the relationship.

There are many ways to nurture a professional relationship. Below are some of the ways that I found success over the years.

- **Handwritten Notes** – In the age of technology the presence of handwritten notes is almost obsolete. Let's face it, it's much easier for you to just type a quick email and hit the send button. This is more of a reason to send a nice, short handwritten note. The recipient also recognizes that it would have been much easier to send an email, BUT you took the time to purchase the stationery, hand-write the note, purchase a stamp, and drop it in the mail.

My experience has been that this type of interaction is a bit more personal than email and, in many cases, more effective. I absolutely love receiving handwritten notes, and I keep all of them. Whether it's someone that has attended one of my seminars, someone that I have assisted in finding a job opportunity (as a referral), or someone that I have placed into a new job opportunity, I keep all handwritten notes as reminders that I'm making a positive impact in someone's life and they were thoughtful enough to share that impact with me.

- **Articles** – Sending an article of interest to someone that you've recently met is a great way to build and nurture a relationship. For example, if you have a business meeting at someone's office and you notice they have a passion for football because they have tons of football memorabilia around the office (photos, a helmet, framed tickets, flags, and pins). You realize that they have an interest in one team specifically and make a mental note of that information.

You later read the newspaper and there is an article about that specific team or a player on that team, make a copy of the article and send it via mail (or scan it and send it via email) to the individual with a simple note that says: "*Hi Dan, I thought you might be interested in the attached. It's a great article about Donovan McNabb. Hope all is well with you. Let's connect soon for lunch.*"

The note is short and simple, and it shows that you were thinking of the recipient without selfish intention.

- **Magazine Subscriptions** - A few years back, I met with a client in my office to discuss their recruiting needs. He arrived just a little bit earlier than the time that we had scheduled, and I wasn't quite ready for our meeting. He entertained himself by reading one of the magazines in the lobby. When I came out to the lobby to get him, I noticed that he still had the magazine in his hand. After we discussed his recruiting needs and our meeting was concluding, he asked if he could take the magazine with him because there were a couple of articles that caught his eye that he wanted to read later. I encouraged him to take the magazine with him and thanked him for the opportunity to do business with him. As soon as he left my office, I ordered him a subscription to that magazine. It was a one-year subscription that cost me $36. Remember, the benefits outweigh the cost. I had just made a deposit into our business relationship.

Every time he received that magazine, he would, of course, think about me and my company. When he received his first copy of the magazine, he called me immediately to thank me and to let me know how thoughtful I was. He asked when would be a good time for us to get together for lunch because he had a couple of referrals for me! A genuine and sincere gesture turned into multiple clients for me! I'm not suggesting that you purchase a magazine subscription for everyone that you come in contact with. I am suggesting that you be cognizant of the things that are important to the individual that you're networking with.

- **Birthday Cards** – When was the last time that you sent a birthday card to someone that you do business with? Birthdays are special for most people. It's their own personal holiday. I'm a HUGE birthday person. I love birthdays! If I know when my client's birthdays are, I store it in my Blackberry and I set it to reoccur. I set a reminder for one week prior so that I can purchase a card and send it out to arrive on or before their birthday. Most of my clients or individuals in my network are on Facebook or LinkedIn, which allows me to see when their birthday is. I don't send a card to everyone in my network as you might imagine, but it certainly is a special touch.

46

Now that you received some tips on various ways to follow up, let's discuss what would happen if you didn't follow up. Imagine for a minute that you meet someone at an event and you never follow up with them. Six months after your initial meeting, you find yourself in a position where you need their assistance. You dig their business card out of your drawer and give them a call. Imagine if you were the person on the receiving end of that call. How receptive would you be if you haven't heard from this person since your initial meeting six months ago? You probably wouldn't be very receptive. Neither will the person on the other end of your call.

You haven't taken the time to build, nurture, and maintain the relationship. In fact, they may not even remember who you are. It may be difficult to reach out to someone and ask for something based on meeting them six months ago and they don't remember who you are. That would be embarrassing, indeed. Let's not place ourselves in that situation!

Just as important as it is to follow up, it is equally as important to follow through. If, for example, you are at a networking event and you mention an article, a book, or a link to a website that you promise to send to that person you have just met, it's important that you do just that. Your reputation, your word, and your credibility are on the line. Should you not follow through on the information that you said you would pass along, that is exactly how the contact will remember you. They will remember that you didn't keep your word and that you didn't follow through on your promise. This is not the best way to start off a relationship.

You don't want to bump into that person at the next networking event and avoid them because you are embarrassed for not delivering on your promise. No one wants to hear a million excuses because you forgot. So, why not put your best foot forward and not only follow up, but follow through. Do what you said you would do. Create a lasting impression on the recipient and you will be on your way toward building a lasting business relationship.

Life is 10% of what happens to you and 90% of how you react to it.
~ John C. Maxwell

7

How to Have a Magnetic Personality

Ever notice how some people just seem to draw others to them? Wouldn't that make networking that much easier? Wouldn't it make a lot less work for you if others were drawn to you like a magnet? I have a magnetic personality and it is something that I have had to work at over the years. I wasn't born with it, and it didn't come naturally. Believe it or not, I wasn't always the social butterfly and Chatter-Kathy that I am today. It was a learned behavior. Some people just naturally have a magnetic personality and others, like me, have to work at it. Because I've been working at it for so many years, it is natural to me now.

In this chapter, you will learn how to draw others to you like a magnet. You will learn techniques that will aid in breaking down the communication barrier by attracting people to you and not repelling them.

Did you know that over 50% of your communication is being conveyed via your body language? Do you know how you are being perceived just by the folding of your arms? How about the way that you tilt your head or how firm you shake hands? What do any of these have to do with networking? Folding your arms across your chest conveys a nervous, negative and even aggressive attitude. Folded arms are an indication that you are not open and perhaps even stand-offish. I'm sure that you don't want to come across like that at a networking event. When I'm at networking events and I extend my hand, and the other person (mostly women) grab the tips of my fingers, I am offended. It's as if the person doesn't want to shake my hand. Oftentimes, it's the exact opposite with me. Many seem to forget that I'm a lady and they squeeze my hand so hard that it hurts. You know the "G.I. Joe with the Kung-Fu grip" handshake.

My mom used to say, "Knowing is half the battle." Now that you know how your body language can be received by others, make a conscious effort to correct any areas that may cause others to view you as unfriendly or unapproachable.

Speaking of body language, I used to be the person standing in the back of the room, hoping that no one would approach me and begin a conversation. I was the person on the airplane praying that whoever sat next to me would not want to talk to me. I was the person at an event that only engaged in dialogue with the person that I came with or people that I already knew. My body language was indicative of my thoughts and lack of desire to engage in dialogue, and as a result, I didn't. People didn't approach me unless it was to say, "Stop looking so mean!" or "It can't be that bad."

This is what my body language conveyed to those around me. This was the exact opposite of magnetism. I was actually repelling people.

I remember my mom saying to me, "You'll get more flies with honey than you will with vinegar." So, I began to apply honey to all of my interactions with people. My goal was to draw people to me, not repel them, and I realized that honey would do that more effectively than vinegar would.

So let's talk about what a magnetic personality looks like. People that have magnetic personalities seem to have some common factors:

- Friendly demeanor
- Genuine interest/concern for others
- Friendly smile
- Humorous
- "The life of the party" kind of personality
- Always make eye contact

It's much easier to approach someone that embodies these elements versus someone that:

- Is frowning
- Looks upset/angry
- Looks bored
- Has folded arms

- Is completely engulfed in their Blackberry or iPhone
- Is wearing their "Don't Talk To Me" T-Shirt

I find that it would be much easier for me to approach someone with the first set of attributes versus the second set. It is also easier for someone to approach me if I embody the magnetic attributes versus the others.

Be conscious of your body language; it screams volumes to others about your demeanor. If you are standing in a corner with your arms folded looking uninterested, the likelihood of someone approaching you to initiate dialogue is slim to none. The same is true if your head is down while on your phone texting or on one of the social networking sites. The only eye contact that you are making is with your phone. You can't establish, nurture and grow a relationship with your phone.

On the opposite side of that, if you have a warm, friendly and inviting smile, and you are comfortable making eye contact, the likelihood of someone approaching you, and engaging you in dialogue, has increased significantly. Your body language is conveying a positive message about you without you saying a word. It also speaks to your confidence. You are beginning to draw others to you like a magnet.

Shoot for the moon. Even if you miss, you'll land among the stars.
~ Les Brown

8

Develop a Strategy: Do Your Research

Plan your work and work your plan! That's right; develop a plan prior to attending any networking event. Brainstorm prior to and think about what you would like to accomplish at this event.

Here are some items for you to consider:
1. Who is sponsoring the event?
2. Who will be attending the event?
3. Who is the keynote speaker?
4. How do I develop a plan of action?

Before you attend a networking event, gather information prior to the event to help you develop a strategy to maximize your time while there. Answering the 4 questions above will aid in developing a plan.

1. **Find out who is sponsoring the event.** Is it an individual, a company, a professional organization, or a school? If it's not an individual, find out who the key players are behind the particular organization. Can these individuals be a resource to you or can you be a resource to them? Having knowledge about the individual or group that is hosting or sponsoring the event will also aid you in initiating conversation with a stranger at the event. You will appear to be "in the know".

2. **Next, let's find out who will be attending the event.** Who is on the dais? Will there be individuals from the political community? Will there be industry leaders? Will there be hiring managers? Will there be partners or CEOs? Find out beforehand who will be attending, and this will help you decide who you want to make contact with. This will help you be more strategic in your networking and maximize the time spent at the networking event. You don't want to walk around aimlessly at the event trying to figure out whom to talk to, that won't be the best use of your time.

   In order to find out vital information beforehand, if there are well-known key players expected at the event, the sponsor may use their names to advertise for the event in an effort to draw a larger crowd. If there is a flyer for the event, the fliers may have a website that you can visit to obtain additional information. Visit the website! You may be surprised at the additional information you find there.

3. **Gather information about the keynote speaker.** If you are afforded an opportunity to dialogue with this individual, it will be very useful to you to have some background knowledge about who they are, what they do, what books they may have written (if any), what industry they are in, and what key accomplishments they have achieved. Find out as much information about the speaker as you can. This information can also serve as a conversation starter with other attendees at the event

4. **Develop a Plan of Action.** After you research the event, make a list of the people that you would like to connect with. Even if you were not able to obtain a list of the attendees, make a list of how many people you would like to connect with, and develop a plan of action from that list. If the event is one-hour long, be strategic, and decide how many people you would like to connect with in that timeframe. If your goal is to make six connections during the hour, that averages out to 10 minutes per person. Generally speaking, at a networking event, you wouldn't spend 10 minutes talking with one person. You're monopolizing their time, and not maximizing yours. Keep in mind that they are there to network and may have a goal in mind as well. Please be considerate of other people's time.

If opportunity doesn't knock, build a door.
~ Milton Berle

9

Be a Resource: It's Not About You!

Many people unfortunately approach networking with the "what's-in-it-for-me" attitude. This mindset will not serve you well in building, nurturing, and maintaining relationships. The biggest misconception about networking is that networking is all about what someone can do for you. It's not about YOU! You will find, as you practice the principles that you've learned thus far, that you will be much more successful at the art of networking when you first seek to be a resource to others.

I had a gentleman aggressively pursuing me about a network marketing opportunity. I had heard all that I wanted to hear about network marketing from him and the others that preceded him, and I had no interest whatsoever in pursuing any opportunities in that industry. I bumped into him a couple of times at various venues since we lived in the same vicinity. Whenever I saw him, I thought, "Here we go again… He's going to try to sell me on this network marketing thing." I didn't give him the time of day or the opportunity to "pitch" anything to me. I wasn't rude to him. I was polite in my small chit-chat, and he was wise enough not to push any further.

He knew that I was a recruiter and I was always looking for talented individuals for various openings. One day, he engaged me on Facebook and inquired if I still had openings in my office that I was seeking to fill. As a matter of fact, I did. I was looking for an office manager. I gave him all of the specifications for the position and within one hour, he provided me with the names and numbers of four candidates with the qualifications that I was looking for. Over the course of the next couple of days, I followed up with the four candidates and two of them were actually a great match. I invited them out for an interview.

Now, let's examine what *really* happened here. His approach with me regarding the multi-level marketing opportunity did not work. I was completely tuned out and not open to hearing anything about it whatsoever. So, he took a different approach. He decided to see how he could be a resource to me, which would in turn make me feel a sense of obligation to at least listen to what he had to say. It worked! You know the old "scratch my back and I'll scratch yours" approach. After I went through the interview process with the candidates that he sent me (I actually ended up hiring a candidate that I found on my own), I reached out to him to thank him for his assistance, provide him with some feedback, and let him know that I had made a decision to hire someone else. About a week or so later, he reached out to me on Facebook again and asked if he could meet with me for 20 minutes to share a business opportunity with me. How could I say no? He came to my office later in the week and introduced me to ZamZuu, and I joined immediately!

What's important to note here is that when you first seek how you can be a resource to others, you will ultimately benefit in the long run. If you're not sure how you can be a resource to someone, just ask them. After you have engaged in small chit-chat, exchanged business cards, and pitched your 30-second elevator speech, simply ask, "How can I be a resource to you?" or "how can I help you grow your business?" This approach will enable you to effectively build the relationship and increase your likelihood for success. When people realize that you are open to helping them, they will be open to helping you.

If you want things to be different, perhaps the answer is to become different yourself.
~Norman Vincent Peale

10

Become Known as a Connecter – Don't be Selfish With Your Network

The very essence of networking itself is establishing, building, nurturing, and maintaining relationships for the purpose of connecting people, whether the connection is for your personal benefit, the personal benefit of the other individual, or the personal benefit of a third or fourth party. Keep in mind, every person that you connect with or build a relationship with may not necessarily be a resource to you specifically, and that's okay. You may indeed be a resource to someone that is close to them, like their spouse, child, their niece or nephew, co-worker, or business partner. This is what I mean by becoming a connector.

In my years of networking, I have noticed that some people are selfish or overly protective of their network. After all, isn't networking about connecting the dots? I'm not sure where the selfish mentality comes from, but maybe people make assumptions and judgments about the value that the other person may bring to their existing network and therefore, are reluctant to connect-the-dots. Or, they don't truly understand the power and purpose of networking themselves. In effect, they have made a decision on behalf of someone that is in their circle instead of allowing the person to make the decision on their own. I am not suggesting that your network, that you've worked hard to establish and maintain, be open to just anyone and everyone, as there needs to be an eliminating process. I am suggesting however, that we take a long hard look at one of the most critical components of this thing called networking, and that's becoming a connector.

When I worked at Arthur Andersen several years ago, I was beginning my transition into recruiting at that time, having attended several out-of-state recruiting events on behalf of the firm. Although I worked in Global Tax & International HR, I made several contacts across the US. I also held a leadership position with a professional organization that had 49 chapters across the US, which meant that I had access to hundreds of people in 49 states. I attended their regional meetings, national meetings, and the national convention. I utilized all of the principles that you have learned thus far in previous chapters. I introduced myself to new people, I let them know who I was, what I did, and I asked them how I could be a resource to them. After the event, I followed up within 48 hours of our meeting or within 48 hours of my return home from these trips. I built a relationship and stayed in contact.

What began to happen is that whenever I had dialogue with someone at a networking event, and they indicated that they were looking to relocate, looking to change jobs, or looking to serve on the board of an organization, I had a contact for them. I had a connection in North Carolina. I had a connection at Chrysler that was in a position to make hiring decisions and was willing to receive referrals from me. I served on the Board of Directors with an individual that also served on the board of another organization that the person that I was speaking with, wanted to serve on. So, I connected the dots! I connected the person that was looking to relocate to my contacts in the area. If I knew a recruiter in that area, I would connect them with the recruiter. If I had a contact at a specific company that they were interested in, I forwarded the resume myself and asked my contact to reach out to the candidate or asked if it were alright for me to give their contact information to the candidate. Please note that I only attached my name (i.e. stamp of approval) to people whose qualification that I knew personally.

This is networking at its best! When you become known as a connector, everyone wants to be in your circle because they know that you have the ability to connect the dots and make things happen! For me, this was done with no selfish intentions. There was no monetary gain or favors provided for me connecting two people who could, and oftentimes would, be a resource for one another. My satisfaction came in knowing that I was able to assist someone else, especially as it relates to a job opportunity. I felt really good about being a connector. That was one of the greatest rewards for me. I didn't mind sharing my network because I was in a position to help others.

As a result of me being a connector, when I need to reach out to any of the individuals that I was able to be a resource to, they will be more than willing to be a resource to me. For example, I introduced a lady named Michelle to my network in North Carolina, which is where she wanted to relocate to be closer to family. She accepted a job opportunity that was introduced to her because of the person I introduced her to. Michelle follows up to thank me and lets me know how everything panned out. She was very happy with the offer that she received and the fact that the company paid her relocation costs. She was now 15 minutes away from her family. I congratulated Michelle and wished her well in her new employment opportunity. Not only did I ask her to stay in touch with me and let me know how things were progressing, but also to let me know how and if I could be a resource to her in the future. I also followed up with my contact in North Carolina that made this job opportunity for Michelle become a reality. I also encouraged him to let me know if I could be a resource to him in the future.

So, my niece wants to attend North Carolina State University because that's the school that her best friend is attending. Both young ladies are looking for internships while in school, and guess who is the first person that comes to my mind? You guessed it right... Michelle! Michelle and I remained in contact and she is now in a senior management position within the organization. I reached out to her on behalf of my niece and her best friend. Michelle was very eager to assist me, as I was to assist her when she reached out. Upon receipt of their resumes, she immediately took them to *her* contact in Human Resources. The rest is well, as they say, history. My niece and her best friend were hired as summer interns at the firm.

This is the power of networking! My niece and her friend were able to prosper as a result of my unselfish willingness to help someone else. That gesture allowed me to positively impact the lives of four people:

1. My contact in North Carolina that was able to be a resource to Michelle. It cast him in a positive light because he was able to introduce a stellar candidate to someone in his circle.
2. It impacted Michelle's life because she not only was able to secure an exciting job and get reimbursement for her relocation costs, but she also was able to move closer to her family, which was her ultimate goal.
3. It impacted the life of my niece as she was able to secure an internship and be closer to her best friend.
4. It impacted my niece's best friend because she too was able to secure an internship.

So, now you can clearly see how powerful networking can be and the positive snowball effect that it can create. So please don't be selfish with your network, you would be defeating the whole purpose of networking. Become known as a connector, and it will help you expand your existing network. This will inadvertently give you good favor with those in your network because you become a valuable resource to them. Always remember, there is no dollar amount that can be placed on the value of a relationship that has been built, nurtured, and maintained.

If we're growing, we're always going to be out of our comfort zone.
~John C. Maxwell

11

Who Should You Network With?

This question seems simple, yet there are a few different answers to this question.

1. It depends on what industry you are in. For example, if you're in the direct sales industry or more specifically, network marketing, the answer to this question would be EVERYONE that you come in contact with. Each individual that you come in contact with can be a potential consumer for the product that you are marketing. Even if they don't join your marketing

business, they can still become a consumer of your product.

2. If you are a professional in a specific industry, I would recommend concentrating your networking efforts (initially) on the specific industry that you are in. For example, if you're an accountant, you may want to concentrate your networking efforts on professional accounting organizations such as the American Institute of Certified Public Accounts (AICPA), or if you're in Michigan, perhaps the Michigan Association of Certified Public Accountants (MACPA). If you're a minority in this industry, you may want to also focus on organizations such as the National Association of Black Accountants (NABA) or perhaps Association of Latino Professionals in Finance and Accounting (ALPFA) or Ascend. The individuals that you will meet as a result of attending various networking events organized by these organizations can potentially yield a strong return on your investment in the future. These individuals are your colleagues in the industry, which means that more than likely, you will run into them at future events and possibly be sitting across the table from them in an interview in the future.

3. You'll also want to focus some efforts with the organizations or companies that support these various professional organizations mentioned above. For accountants, it would certainly be the Big 4 accounting firms, the regional or local accounting firms, and any of the major organizations that support the initiatives of these professional organizations. General Motors and McDonald's are two examples. Network in the arena where you have an opportunity to engage individuals that are specific to your industry.

Whether you think you can or think you can't... you are right!
~ Henry Ford

12

Networking Techniques for Introverts

L et's face it, not all of us were born with the "networking" gene, and not all of us come from a background where our parents were professional networkers and could teach us the ropes or the rules of engagement. For many of us, networking is a learned behavior. We either had to teach ourselves (trial-by-fire) or take classes, seminars, workshops, or read a book or two on networking, like what you're doing right now.

Believe it or not, the author (that would be me!) was NOT a natural networker. It was something that I had to learn over the course of the years. After many years of consistent practice and study (from reading materials), I began to perfect my craft as I saw all of the benefits that were a direct result of networking itself. The way in which I learned was by observing my colleagues while in the office or at various after-work networking events. Some people just seemed to be the life of the party.

I watched the ease with which the people who were the life of the party approached other people. I observed their body language, their posture, their attire, and their hair and make-up. I made it a point to observe the entire networking dynamic. I noticed how much time was spent with each potential contact. I made note of how the conversation was started, what was discussed and what was avoided in discussion. In many instances, I was able to observe (and sometimes participate in) the dialogue that was taking place and take mental notes on the who, what, how, when, and why. I gravitated toward the "life-of-the-partiers" because I wanted to emulate their behavior, and what I believed to be their success. Basically, I attached myself to the extrovert(s) in the room.

Extroverts seem to have a natural sense of ease when approaching a perfect stranger and engaging him/her in conversation. That's what I wanted to learn how to do. The best way, I figured, to learn how to do what they did was to become joined at the hip with the extrovert and emulate their behavior. It's like an actor studying for the part of a homeless character in a major motion picture. I had to become an extrovert! I had to study their movement, their various styles, their language, and the way in which they began a conversation. What better way for me to get into character than to hang around, study, and learn from an extrovert.

During my transformation process, I decided to let the hard-working extrovert work for me. What I discovered was that extroverts are oftentimes "connectors". They are the person that knows everyone else. So in my attachment to the extrovert at any given event, the extrovert naturally introduced me to their network and therefore, broke the ice for me.

Extroverts seemed to understand this whole networking phenomenon. They would naturally introduce me to whomever they were speaking with. This would play itself out in either one of two ways. The extrovert would either be approached while we were in conversation, and they would say, *"Bob, have you met Tammy? Tammy is a recruiter at XYZ Company, and she is looking for some sharp entry-level accountants."* The conversation would progress from there. The extrovert actually made the initial contact for me. This area of networking, how to initiate conversation, is the one that frightens people the most.

The other way that the "attach yourself to an extrovert" scenario plays out is when you (the introvert) are engaged in dialogue and the extrovert sees someone in the room whom they feel that you should "connect" with and they may say to you, *"Tammy, let me take you over here and meet Bob. Bob is the HR Director at XYZ Company and I know that he is looking for some accountants right now and perhaps the two of you can be a resource to one another."* Then they make the connection and you're starting out the conversation with the credibility that the extrovert's introduction has given you.

The only way that both of these scenarios will work is if the extrovert knows who you are, what you do, and how you can be a resource to someone in their network or vice versa. Extroverts, in my experience, are natural connectors and won't mind being a resource to you and "showing you the ropes".

Once the connection is made however, it's up to you to follow up and follow through.

Networking Challenge:

Find out who the extroverts are and have them help you break the ice at your next networking event.

The only limitations that we have are the ones that we place on our own mind.
~Tammy L. Turner

13

Networking within Your Current Company

Have you ever been invited to a company outing, picnic, or after-work affair and you dreaded the very thought of going? Have you ever felt that you would have nothing in common with your colleagues or just didn't want to socialize with them outside of the office?

If you answered "yes" to either or both of the questions above, this chapter is for you.

Many people have the mistaken belief that networking begins once you leave the office or at a particular outside event. This could not be further from the truth. You have a wealth of resources and contacts at your fingertips. They are called co-workers! Yes, that's right. Your colleagues are a valuable resource to you in developing and growing your professional network.

Most of your colleagues are familiar faces to you, unless you work for a large firm or you are contracted out on various assignments. Because they are familiar faces, the fear of approaching a complete stranger is minimized slightly. If nothing else, you can immediately identify your common bond--you work for the same company.

Before we discuss actual techniques for engaging colleagues at work, let's discuss why this is important in the first place. As I mentioned in Chapter 1, my first experience with networking within my office was at my first job in Corporate America. The firm had many different teams (divisions), and these teams socialized frequently outside of the company at team outings.

Now let's pause for a moment and reflect on why a Fortune 100 company saw the need or importance of employees interacting with one another outside of the workplace. It was to encourage and promote team camaraderie, to build team morale, and to have an opportunity to connect with colleagues in a different setting; one that is relaxed, comfortable, and void of the stresses of the office. It also created an environment where titles were irrelevant, which would inevitably allow everyone to relax. The team outings would bring the team together at events such as the Detroit Tigers Opening Day game, Whirlyball, Bowling, Firm Softball Team, Detroit Pistons games, Detroit Lions games, and even Happy Hour at the local brewery.

All of these activities were supported financially by the firm. They basically paid us to go out and have fun "networking" with our colleagues. It was incorporated into the budget because they understood that you spend more time with people that you work with than anyone else and, as a result, you want to foster a team environment, a family environment, and an environment where you feel comfortable.

I can see why companies would incorporate this in the budget. It absolutely worked! Another company that I worked for later in my career seemed to have this practice down to a science. Although I can actually say that I never worked for a company that I did not like, I must admit that this particular organization was by far my favorite place to work throughout my career.

What made this company such a wonderful place to work? It was because the employers got "the formula". They understood the following formula: Happy + Employees = Productivity, and the other formula, Unhappy + Employees = Employees on the Internet during work hours looking for new job opportunities, and hence they're unproductive.

This company invested a lot of money into ensuring a comfortable work environment and many opportunities to network with colleagues during office hours and outside of the office. We had give-a-ways to the Pistons Suite, scavenger hunts, marathon-type games, a popcorn machine with free popcorn throughout the day, a Slushie machine, and we had awards ceremonies where awards were given throughout the organization for outstanding performance. We even had black-tie affairs.

As a result of the company investing in these types of activities, the employees were loyal, hard-working, and motivated. This was the type of organization that you were excited to go to every day. How many people can truly say that they're "on fire" about going to work every day, that they're truly excited because they love their job and the company that they work for? In talking with friends and colleagues, it's been more of the opposite, more dreading of going to work versus excitement. These are the reasons that the company invested so much time and money into these various activities--to build camaraderie and to ensure that they had "happy" employees that were ultimately productive. This company was Quicken Loans/Rock Financial in Livonia, Michigan.

Inter-Company Networking Techniques

So, let's discuss some ways to engage your colleagues at work in an effort to expand your existing network.

Invite a Co-Worker To Lunch

Let's start off with something really simple. Invite your co-worker to lunch. If the office that you work in has a cafeteria, have lunch there. If not, invite them to a local, inexpensive restaurant around the office. This affords you the opportunity to learn more about your colleague, their spouse, their interests, their goals, and their network. From this conversation, you can potentially gauge how you can be a resource to them, and how they may be a resource to you. This does not have to be exclusive to only the colleagues in your particular department. Venture outside of your department and get to know colleagues in other areas within the organization.

Join, Lead or Organize a Team or Company Activity

This is an absolutely wonderful way to get to know your colleagues. As we discussed earlier, companies will invest in team activities because of the results that it yields. Here's an opportunity for you to participate on a particular team that is already organized. This gives you the opportunity to network with the planning committee who probably knows everyone within the organization. This will be great exposure for you.

You can volunteer to lead a team or activity within your organization, which will also position you in a place to network not only with colleagues, but company leaders as well. This also allows you to exhibit your leadership skills. Even when you think no one is watching, the company leaders will take notice of your efforts.

Research the non-profit organizations that the company supports, and volunteer to participate. Many organizations support non-profits such as Habitat for Humanity, Paint the Town, and Junior Achievement. Companies take their participation with these organizations very seriously. This is their way of giving back to the community. As a volunteer, you have the opportunity to network with your colleagues while working toward a common goal and supporting the company's community initiatives.

The After-Work Get Together

If you have a family, it's not always easy to make it to these types of gatherings because you need to get the children from latchkey or the babysitter. While you may not be able to attend every company after-work affair, plan to at least attend two of them during the year. This will do wonders for your career. Again, it exposes you to company leadership and it affords you the opportunity to interact and mingle outside of the office. Though it often serves as a time of rest and relaxation, don't underestimate the relationship you could establish simply by attending Happy Hour.

Find a Mentor

Another great way to network within your organization is to find a mentor. Think about the leadership within your organization. Who is in a position within the organization that you would like to be in, in the future? Is this person in the same field that you are in within the organization (HR, Accounting, PR, Graphic Design, etc.)? Connect with this individual at company outings in an effort to build a relationship, or ask another colleague to make an introduction on your behalf. Ask the individual about their goals and why they chose XYZ Company to work for.

Over time, when you've reached a level of comfort with them, ask them to mentor you. Share your vision, dreams, and goals. If the individual agrees to take you on as a mentee, you will have access to them and their network. Because they are your mentor, they will gladly introduce you to their network, this is part of "showing you the ropes". As your mentor, they will educate you on the importance of making certain contacts and connections within the industry. If they currently have those connections, they will more than likely be happy to connect the dots for you.

If the individual that you have chosen to be your mentor happens to be well-connected, people will want to get to know who you are based on the mere fact that you are connected with your mentor. They will be a resource to you based upon that relationship alone.

Should you choose to tap into that network, be very careful to always follow up and follow through because the reputation of your mentor is on the line. If you're tapping into his/her network, it may be a good idea to run the idea past him/her first to ensure you're taking the proper approach and that you're not damaging any relationships along the way.

A pessimist sees the difficulty in every opportunity. An optimist sees the opportunity in every difficulty.
~ Winston Churchill

14

It's Not Kissing UP!

One of the biggest misconceptions about networking is that it is "kissing up" or "sucking up." Networking, by definition, is the process of building, nurturing, and maintaining *mutually beneficial* business relationships. The operative phrase here is "mutually beneficial", which implies that both parties will obtain some type of benefit as a result of this connection. If you're gaining some type of benefit, or able to be of benefit to someone else, how can this possibly be "kissing up"?

When a person attends a networking event, social function or business event, each party is there with the purpose of connecting with people that may be able to be a resource to them or someone that they know. This is understood and is an acceptable business practice. Therefore, you shouldn't be afraid to approach it as such or view networking with such a negative connotation.

As mentioned in previous chapters, networking is the single most effective tool used to advance a person's career, and as an entrepreneur, salesperson, student, or business professional, it is expected that you will learn the art of networking to advance your career, be a resource to others, and grow your business.

Let me offer you this, if you take two individuals with the same education and same level of experience, and all other variables are equal, except one of them has a contact at the potential employer and the other one does not, I can guarantee you that the person that has a contact at that particular company will get the job every time. This is the POWER of networking!

Keep in mind, however, that there is a certain level of responsibility attached to networking. Most savvy business professionals will not attach their name to someone whom they don't feel is a stellar candidate or potential resource to the person with whom they make the recommendation to.

Your network must be able to trust you and the recommendations or referrals that you send them. If you are the referral, protect the reputation of the person that referred you by living up to their recommendations. Not only is your reputation on the line, but the reputation of the person that referred you is on the line as well.

Once you begin to change your negative view of networking, you will be successful at it. With networking, the benefits certainly outweigh the costs.

NETWORKING CHALLENGE:

Draw a line down the middle of a sheet of lined paper. On the top left, write PROS, and on the top right, write CONS. Write down all of the benefits of expanding your network (the pros) and weigh them against the costs (the cons) of expanding your existing network. I can assure you that the pros will outweigh the cons in this scenario. I don't believe you could actually come up with a legitimate con for networking. If you do, let me know.

Don't be fooled though, networking does require work. It requires a commitment to nurture and maintain your relationships, but that is true of any relationship, whether it's business or personal. In the famous words of Thomas Edison, "Opportunity is missed by most people because it comes dressed in overalls and looks like work." Don't let opportunity pass you by because you think it's "kissing up".

Once our minds are tattooed with negative thinking, our chances
for long-term success diminish.
~ John C. Maxwell

15

Don't Be Afraid

Throughout my many years of conducting workshops on networking and business etiquette, through the Q & A sessions, I came across a consistent theme--that many people are afraid of approaching individuals outside of their race. I understood completely where this mindset was derived from, because I too experienced this.

When I first began my career in Corporate America, I too felt a level of comfort around those that looked like me because I felt that they could identify with me more so than those that did not look like me. I wasn't quick to approach people of other cultures because I felt that we didn't have anything in common. I felt that we didn't have the same cultural background, we didn't go to the same schools, we didn't have the same hobbies or interests, and frankly, we didn't have the same problems or challenges. I felt that they couldn't relate to my struggle as a woman, much less an African-American woman.

Because I held onto these fears, I made them a reality in my head and this type of thinking is what prevented me, early in my career, from networking with individuals that didn't look like me.

Wisdom and years of experience have taught me that there is only ONE race... and that is the HUMAN RACE. While we may not have gone to the same schools, had the same cultural background, same religious background, some hobbies or interest, one thing was certain... no matter what race we are, we all put our pants on one leg at a time. Once I came to this conclusion, I began to interact with people differently. I found that across the board, whether black, white, or Asian, other cultures experienced this same fear. What I also realized is that in a social setting, each of us was looking for the other person to "make the first move" and break the ice.

So, while I am holding on to all these fears about talking to someone that I believe has nothing in common with me, people of other cultures were doing the same. If no one took the initiative to make the first move, then the interaction would never take place. Wow! There's a missed opportunity indeed. We live in a world that interacts globally. Therefore, we need to think globally. As an African-American woman, I realize everyone in the world is not African-American and that everyone that I do business with, work with, worship with, and eat with will not be African-American. The same is true of Asians and Whites, women and men. The entire world is not comprised of one culture or one gender. In order to be successful in life, you must learn to interact with those that don't look like you.

While your life experiences may not mirror those of a person in a different culture, you will soon realize that you have more in common than you may have initially realized. After all, one component of networking is finding the common thread.

The HUMAN RACE can also been seen as that common thread. Cast those fears aside and take a genuine interest in people that may be different than you. I challenge you to examine how you can add value and education to their lives, and how they can add to yours. Erase the cultural barriers. It's common to be comfortable with who you are familiar with. But if you never meet new people, you may be missing the business opportunity of a lifetime.

Everything is always created twice; first in the mind, then in reality.
~ Anonymous

16

Social Media Networking

One word: Facebook! It has changed the face of social networking forever. In 2008, social media networking helped elect the first African-American President of the United States. I can actually recall the day that President Obama was inaugurated. I watched the inauguration on CNN in my office with my staff. CNN partnered with Facebook to allow you to connect with millions of users across the world who also watched the inauguration. We had the ability to chat with one another and share stories of how we felt, how our parents felt, and what this milestone meant for Americans living and working in the U.S. and those abroad.

There are a multitude of other social media networking outlets such as MySpace, LinkedIn, Twitter, and blogs. The beauty of these tools is that you have an opportunity to network and meet potential business partners, or reconnect with friends, colleagues, relatives, or former classmates.

These social media networking tools allow the average person to expand their existing network from the comfort of their armchair. This dynamic has given a new face, and oftentimes, a new challenge to networking. The positive aspect is that it allows you to expand your existing network by having the ability to reach people that you would not normally have had an opportunity to interact with. Just as with traditional forms of networking, the key is still building, nurturing, and maintaining the relationships. The core principles of networking don't change, even though the vehicle may have.

The potential negative side of *only* using social media networking as a tool to expand your existing network is that it provides a false sense of security. Allow me to explain. One of the biggest fears of networking is initiating conversation. This fear is due to the fact some people fear rejection, while some simply don't know what to say.

Well, social media networking has effectively eliminated the fear of speaking to a person face-to-face. It is much easier to initiate conversation with someone over the Internet than with someone standing right in front of you. Social media networking provides a false sense of security because it certainly will not empower you to be more comfortable talking face-to-face to strangers.

While I promote and strongly encourage people to utilize social media, do not solely depend on social media as an avenue to expanding your network. There may be people that still prefer the time-tested method of a firm handshake and a smile to become comfortable with you and begin to develop a relationship.

According to www.internetstats.com, as of August 2010, Facebook has over 500 million users with the largest population being in North America and the second largest being Australia! That means that in North America, 1 in every 14 people have a Facebook account! For a business owner, this is a dream come true. What this translates to is FREE access to 500 million potential customers. This means that I also have FREE advertising to 500 million people that I would not normally have access to unless I paid for promotion. Keep in mind that this is from Facebook alone. You still have access to a multitude of other social media outlets.

According to www.mashable.com, 22.7% of all time spent on the Internet is spent on social networking sites. In December of 2009, Twitter processed more than 1 billion tweets and they boast an average of 40 million tweets per day, according to Twitter. Again, this is another powerful tool used to connect with others and expand your network.

I must admit that I have joined the club of those that are addicted to social media, and particularly "Crackbook", as many lovingly call it. I have four Facebook accounts. I maxed out the number of friends that I could have on one account, "Tammy Turn Page One", which is 5,000 friends. So I set up a second page, "Tammy Turn Page Two". I also created a third page where I could connect with people that shared the same spiritual and religious views as I do. I didn't want my professional life to intertwine with my spiritual life; this was my page of refuge from the rest of the world. Last, but not least, I created a Fan Page for this book.

This is how I choose to utilize Facebook; however, people utilize Facebook in a variety of ways. Some people only accept people they know or already have a personal relationship with. I will accept anyone that looks professional and "appears" to be a potential consumer or resource. My philosophy is that I can't expand my network if the ONLY people that I interact with are people that I already know.

Be cautious about the way in which you manage your social media outlets. Please keep in mind that ANY and EVERY thing that you post online, from status updates and pictures, to comments on other people's pages, becomes public knowledge the moment you post it online. Posting information online is like taking out a front page ad in the newspaper.

Recruiters and hiring managers are now utilizing social media sites to screen "out" candidates. When a potential employee applies for a job opportunity, they provide their email address, and that's how recruiters find them on social media outlets. The same email address you use on your resume is more than likely the same email address you use to set up your social media accounts. Now, the point here isn't for you to change email addresses. The point here is that you need to be very cognizant of the information that you share via social media outlets such as Facebook.

Time after time, you hear of someone who was fired from their job due to something they posted on their Facebook page. Think about all the people that were never hired because a recruiter saw something inappropriate on their page. The job of a recruiter is to get to know a candidate. Recruiters want to get a feel for your personality to see if you could potentially be a good fit within their organization. When you go to a job interview, you are going to naturally put your best foot forward. The recruiter has the opportunity to meet your "representative", the YOU that you want the recruiter to believe that you are. The recruiter is then left to their own decisiveness to determine if the "representative" should move to the next phase of the interviewing process.

What social media allows recruiters to do is discover the "real you". So, recruiters go to your social media sites like Facebook, YouTube, and MySpace, and look at your status updates, your wall, your comments, and your videos. This lets them truly see the person that they are considering for employment. Now, if the person that came to the office, the "representative", doesn't match the person on the social media sites, then chances are that you probably won't be invited back for a second interview.

I've seen this happen most frequently with college students. They utilize the sites to connect with their classmates, complain about their professor, and find out where the parties are for the weekend, but oftentimes the language that they use is sometimes vulgar or derogatory. When they find themselves seeking an internship or job after graduation, and the recruiter "Google's" them or finds them on Facebook, or YouTube they have effectively guaranteed that they will NOT get the job based on their prior or current irresponsibility with social media. A couple of years ago, I remember reading about a football executive losing his job based on what he posted on Twitter about the franchise he worked for. The bottom line is: post and interact responsibly.

Social media networking is an absolutely wonderful tool that, when used properly, can grow your business and expand your network; however, you must use it responsibly, especially if you are a job seeker or business owner. Your page is a reflection of your character. Treat it like your business depends on it.

The richest people in the world look for and build networks;
everyone else looks for work.
~ Robert Kiyosaki

17

"*Network*" Marketing

Multi-level marketing has become a rapidly growing industry here in the United States. It has taken us by storm. Let's face it: In the economic times that we are in, lots of people are looking for ways to bring additional income into their homes. The basis of multi-level marketing, or "*Network*" marketing, is relationship-building. In order to experience the maximum success in a "*Network*" marketing opportunity, you need to master the art of networking.

Individuals that have experienced success in this industry would tell you that they have built relationships and have showed their team or downline how to build relationships, and how to nurture, maintain, foster, and support those relationships. Statistics show that consumers buy from people that they like. You are more inclined to take the suggestion or recommendation of someone that you consider a friend or acquaintance versus an absolute stranger.

In most instances with *"Network"* marketing, the business owner generally taps into their own existing network upon entering the business. They approach the individuals that are closest to them, their families, their church members, schoolmates, and fellow colleagues. After they have exhausted these avenues, they seek to engage "strangers", or have individuals in their downlines to introduce them to their existing network.

Again, those that have experienced the most success in this industry have mastered the art of networking and engaging strangers and have used the techniques explained in previous chapters of this book. In order for anyone to expand their existing network, they MUST talk to strangers.

If you are currently in a MLM (Multi-level Marketing), I implore you to use the techniques that you have learned in this book to work on building your existing network. It will do wonders for your business. Keep in mind, the essence of the MLM industry is relationship-building. You can't build relationships if you're not talking to people. Don't just stop with your existing network; get out there and meet new people. ~ Let's go!!

Learn to say "no" to the good, so you can say "yes" to the best.
~ John C. Maxwell

18

Networking Don'ts

Well, we've discussed multiple techniques to assist you in expanding your existing network and/or creating a new network. Now that you're empowered with the tools to be successful at networking, let's take a moment to discuss some of the things you want to be mindful about, and take care not to engage in, while at networking events.

- **Don't monopolize the time of the person that you are speaking with.**

  You always want to be mindful and respectful of the time of the person(s) that you are engaging and interacting with. Keep in mind that the goal is to engage, connect, and follow up and follow through. If you monopolize the time of the individual that you are speaking with, it prevents them from also taking advantage of the opportunity to network with others at the event. It can also possibly make a bad first impression. Maximize your time. Save the lengthy conversation for the follow-up luncheon.

- **Stay engaged with the person that you are speaking with.**
It's very important to give the person that you are speaking with your undivided attention. Be mindful of when you are engaged in dialogue with someone, that you're not constantly looking over their shoulder to see who else is in the room or who else is coming through the door. You could give the other person the impression that they are not important to you or perhaps that they are "less" important than the person that you are looking for. That's not a good first impression and it can actually be viewed as rude.

- **Give the Blackberry a break.**
If you are at a networking event, you're there to interact with individuals and not be engulfed in your phone. If you are engaged in dialogue with someone, but you're constantly reading your text messages or even worse, you are messaging during a conversation, that won't go over very well with the other person. I'm just as addicted to my Blackberry as the next professional; however, I realize that when I'm engaged in conversation with someone, I don't want to come across as rude or uninterested. My suggestion would be to place the phone on silent or vibrate, and in-between conversations or after the event, check it if you must.

- **If you see someone engaged in dialogue, don't just stand there.**
Interrupting an existing conversation can be a bit tricky and at

108

times, awkward. But what's even more awkward is standing outside of a circle of people engaged in conversation, waiting to find an opportunity to jump in. It makes for an uncomfortable situation for those that are having a conversation, and it shows that you may not have much experience at networking. A great way to join an existing conversation is to simply say, "Hey, this looks like an interesting and engaging group here. Mind if I join you? My name is Tammy." More than likely, they will welcome you into the conversation.

- **Never speak ill of a person or a specific company.**
  Once upon a time, there was a belief that there are six degrees of separation. I would argue that in today's society, especially with social media networking, that the separation is closer to two degrees. You never know who knows who, so my recommendation would be to refrain from speaking ill of anyone or any company. The person on the receiving end of the conversation will more than likely view this as being in bad taste and exercising poor judgment. The person that you are actually speaking ill of could in fact be a friend or relative even. The company or organization that you are speaking ill of could in fact be a huge supporter of the individual that you are speaking to. It's best to err on the side of caution on this one, and just don't do it.

- **Don't "name drop".**
  When you're engaged in conversation with someone, resist the urge to impress them by dropping names of prominent individuals that you know or that you may have met before. In my experience, this is not impressive; it's actually viewed as a turn-off.

- **Don't proposition the person that you are speaking with.**
  If you are at a professional networking event, assume that those that are in attendance are there for just that--professional networking--not screening out potential dates.

- **Alcohol consumption.**
  If you are at a networking event where alcohol is being consumed, please be mindful of how much you drink. Remember, first impressions are lasting ones. You don't want to create a bad first impression because of something you said or did that you can't take back or that you don't even remember taking place.

- **Don't forget to keep some mints handy!**

ABOUT THE AUTHOR

Innovative and determined are understatements when it comes to describing Tammy Turner. For her, success is not an option. It is a must. While some know her as the queen of networking, others know her as a phenomenal entrepreneur and community developer. From high school and college students to churches and professional organizations, her mission is clearly to help others obtain the same, or an even higher, level of professional success that she has in her career thus far.

After serving for over six years in the field of public accounting, having worked at major firms such as Arthur Andersen and Deloitte & Touche, Tammy realized that her true passion was in the field of Human Resources. More specifically, she wanted to personally help place people in various positions of employment. As such, Tammy worked as a recruiter for Robert Half Finance & Accounting and a senior recruiter at Quicken Loans/Rock Financial. In 2004, Tammy was able to travel overseas to Cambodia where she worked at the International School of Phnom Penh (ISPP) and as a recruiting consultant for UNICEF and HR, Inc. Cambodia. The experience and training over those two and a half years catapulted her into starting her *own* professional recruiting business, International Employment Solutions, in 2006.

After her return to the United States in 2007, Tammy was able to launch her second recruiting business, Kapstone Recruiting & Training Services, LLC. Seeking to grow the business globally, she has aspirations to open another Kapstone Recruiting office in Singapore in 2012. Her *Elements of Success* program has helped shape the careers of students and business professionals throughout the U.S. and abroad. In this program, she offers resume writing techniques, business etiquette tips, interviewing tips, and skills to successfully master the art of networking. Her debut book, *How to Talk to Strangers: A Step-by-Step Guide to Professional Networking*, is a vital tool for any business professional looking to go to the next level. Your mother may have told you not to talk to strangers, but Tammy teaches you *how* to talk to them.

For speaking engagements or to order additional copies of How to Talk to Strangers, please visit www.MyTammyTurner.com or email info@MyTammyTurner.com

CPSIA information can be obtained at www.ICGtesting.com
Printed in the USA
266934BV00001B/7/P